Thank you
for getting our book!

⭐⭐⭐⭐⭐

**If you found this book
fun and educational, we would be very grateful
if you posted a short review on Amazon!**

MW01132002

Rosa Parks

Isn't it amazing to ride the bus? You get to look out the window and talk with your friends, but bus rides weren't always fun for everyone. In the past, white and black people had to sit separately on the bus...weird, isn't it?! One day, a brave lady stood up and said "NO" she refused to sit away from white people because she saw no difference between her and them – she believed everyone is equal, and they are! Rosa Parks made it possible for anyone to sit wherever they want, regardless of the colour of their skin.

Martin Luther King, Jr.

Martin Luther King, Jr. was FEARLESS! He stopped at nothing to achieve racial justice for EVERYONE. The most powerful tool he possessed was his VOICE! He became one of the most famous speakers of all time because he used words to create change, and he ALWAYS spoke from his heart. Do you have a dream like Martin Luther King, Jr.?

Maya Angelou

Maya Angelou had a real-life superpower, do you know what it was? It was her words! She used words like magic, to cast spells over people and make them see things differently. She had a special gift. She wrote lots, and lots of books about freedom, love and embracing the colour of your skin. She once said, "If you don't like something, change it. If you can't change it, change your attitude"...you always have the power to change things if you really, REALLY want to!

Malcolm X

Just like the letter in the alphabet, his second name is X! Malcolm X stood passionately against the discrimination of black people, he refused to let the bullies hurt other people. He even went to jail because he was so passionate! One of his friends was Martin Luther King, Jr., and they fought together as friends for the same dream. A dream where white and black people lived together peacefully and happily! Malcolm said, "Education is the passport to the future"...so, keep learning!

Nina Simone

Are you FEELING GOOD? Nina Simone makes music that makes everyone feel good! Her songs are all about black representation and standing up for justice for all. You might have heard her song on Halloween, when the radio plays one of her famous songs *I Put a Spell on You*...and she really does put a spell on everyone with her music! Her voice is powerful, it's strong and it changed the history of music forever. Nina said, "I'll tell you what freedom is to me. No fear"...so, remember, be FEARLESS!

Jackie Robinson

Do you like baseball? Well, Jackie Robinson LOVED baseball! He was the first ever black athlete to play Major League Baseball for the Brooklyn Dodgers...cool, right?! But, he didn't only play baseball, he helped fight for the rights of every American. Because he believed that everyone deserves equality and freedom. Just like when he said, "There's not an American in this country free until every one of us is free"...because freedom is freedom for ALL!

Mae Jemison

Mae Jemison spent lots of time looking at the stars. She LOVED space! When she grew up, she became the first African American female astronaut and was the FIRST African American woman in space. How COOL is that?! Do you like to look at the stars like Mae?

Frederick Douglass

Frederick Douglass shows us that ANYTHING is possible. He was a slave before becoming a politician and writer...he proved that NO matter where you come from, what your life may be like, there is ALWAYS a way to change things! He wrote about change and equality between white and black people his whole life - it was his biggest dream. So, use YOUR voice for change because the world wants to hear YOU!

Ella Baker

Ella Baker cared about making the world a better place, so she worked at creating justice and equality for all Black Americans. She was good friends with Martin Luther King, Jr. and together, they used their voices to make change! Although, the most important thing to Ella was that everyone protested peacefully, because she didn't believe in violence but instead, she believed in love bringing people together.

James Baldwin

James Baldwin loved to write, he loved it SO much! He believed that books had this magical power that could help make the bad things in life better. He wrote about race, spirituality and about how humans should come together despite their differences. Isn't the world a better place when we all work together? He said, "Be careful what you set your heart upon - for it will surely be yours"...dreams really can come true!

Harriet Tubman

The best two words to describe Harriet Tubman are, **STRONG** and **FEARLESS**. She escaped from slavery and then she made it her mission to free other slaves. She believed that she was not free until **EVERYONE** was free. Freedom is not about just one person, but a whole group of people! She once said the powerful words, "Don't ever stop. Keep going. If you want a taste of freedom, keep going." **NEVER GIVE UP!**

Jean-Michel Basquait

Do you like to draw or paint? Well, Jean-Michel Basquait made art his whole life! He was really, REALLY good at it! When he was younger, he used to draw all over the paper he would find in his house, it made him so happy that he decided he wanted to be an artist. To Jean, art was the most beautiful thing in the world and one of the most beautiful ways to show-off black cultures!

Jimi Hendrix

Jimi Hendrix was **AMAZING** at playing the guitar, everyone in the **WHOLE** world knows his music! He believed that music could help heal and most importantly, make people happy! He once said, "When the power of love overcomes the love of power, the world will have peace." So, he practiced every day at playing guitar so he could help create peace through his music. He shows us that practice really does make perfect!

Nefertiti

Nefertiti was an Egyptian queen! A long, long time ago, she and her husband were very important people in society and was admired by ALL. In the past, you couldn't take photos so there are no photos of her; but in Berlin, there's a sculpture of her and you can see her REALLY beautiful crown!

Kobe Bryant

Kobe Byrant is a friend of Michael Jordan, and they both play basketball. He was SO good at basketball that he even won FIVE NBA titles! Kobe was also passionate about allowing ALL little boys and girls play basketball that he opened his own summer camp called, *Kobe Basketball Academy* where you could go and train to be just like him!

Stevie Wonder

Stevie loves to create WONDERful songs! He plays the piano as well as singing, and he proves that even when you are blind you are NOT limited in what you can do! His music is full of pure heart and soul - it's magical. Music, in his opinion, means "Music, at its essence, is what gives us memories. And the longer the song has existed in our lives, the more memories we have of it." Keep making memories!

Bob Marley

Now...Bob Marley is perhaps the funkiest singer EVER! His songs are all about LOVE, HOPE and FREEDOM! He views ALL people as the same and united by their hearts, not their differences. His music is amazing to listen to when you want to dance, or when you want to be calm...he has a song for EVERYTHING!

Tutankhamun

King Tut was an Egyptian pharaoh who became a king when he was only **NINE**! One day, some archaeologists found his tomb which is now one of the most famous tombs in the world! Do you know anything about Egyptians like King Tut?

Thank you
for getting our book!

If you found this book fun and educational, we would be very grateful if you posted a short review on Amazon! Your support does make a difference and we read every review personally.

If you would like to leave a review, just head on over to this book's Amazon page and click "Write a customer review".

Thank you for your support!

Made in the USA
Las Vegas, NV
20 February 2024

86017357R00024